In Your
Seventies
and Still Having Fun!

THIS IS A PRION BOOK

First published in Great Britain in 2016 by Prion
An imprint of the Carlton Publishing Group
20 Mortimer Street
London W1T 3JW

A CIP catalogue for this book is available from the British Library.

ISBN 978-1-85375-958-1

Printed in Dubai

10 9 8 7 6 5 4 3 2

In Your
Seventies
and Still Having Fun!

Humorous and Inspirational Quotes
for those Aged 70 and Beyond

PRION

Contents

Life Begins at 70   9

Life is a Funny Old Thing   37

Mind, Body and Soul   65

Terms and Conditions Apply   91

Seventy Ain't for Sissies   117

Introduction

In these infant years of the 21st century, growing old isn't as old-fashioned as it used to be.

'Seventy is the new 40' is now a phrase you'll often hear bandied between a gaggle of gossiping septuagenarians among hipster coffee spots and classy designer shops up and down the country. And it's true. Gone are the days of fusty old farts sitting in dusty old sheds drearily wishing their life away while cleaning the bins – and good riddance! These days, grannies and grandpas are called 'silver foxes' and 'golden agers' and can be seen having twice as much fun as those miserable young people constantly looking down at their stupid smartphones.

So, toss away your walking stick, ditch your bi-focals and stop looking for your spectacles (they're on your head, FYI), and start cracking on with having even more fun than ever before.

Life Begins
at 70

"Thank God! Now I realize
I've been chained to an idiot
for the last 60 years of my life!"

Kingsley Amis, on his lost libido

"Being 70 is not a sin."

Golda Meir

"I am now 70, rather glad, really,
that I won't live to see the horrors
to come in the 21st century."

Anne Stevenson

"At 20 a man is full of fight and hope. He wants to reform the world. When he is 70 he still wants to reform the world, but he knows he can't."

Rodney Dangerfield

"To be 70 years young is sometimes far more cheerful and hopeful than to be 40 years old."

Oliver Wendell Holmes

"I think a lot about getting old. I don't want to be one of those 70-year-olds who still want lots of sex."

Rupert Everett

"Oh, to be 70 again."

Georges Clemenceau

——"If it's true that 50 is the new 30, then it follows that 70 is the new 50."

Joan Collins

"When you are 40, half of you belongs to the past... And when you are 70, nearly all of you."

Jean Anouilh

"You don't realize what fine fighting material there is in old age. You show me anyone who's lived to over 70 and you show me a fighter – someone who's got the will to live."

Agatha Christie

"I shall not die young,
for I am already near 70:
I may die old."

Laurence Housman

"I have achieved my 70 years in
the usual way, by sticking strictly to
a scheme of life which would kill
anybody else... I will offer here, as
a sound maxim, this: that we can't
reach old age by another man's road."

Mark Twain

"On my 70th birthday I felt as if
I were standing on a mountain
height, at whose foot the ocean of
eternity was audibly rushing; while
before me, life with its deserts and
flower-gardens, its sunny days and
its stormy days, spread out green,
wild and beautiful."

Heinrich Zschokke

"The years between 50 and 70 are the hardest. You are always being asked to do more, and you are not yet decrepit enough to turn them down."

T. S. Eliot

"Many people die at 25 and aren't buried until they are 75."

Benjamin Franklin

"The great secret that all old people share is that you really haven't changed in 70 or 80 years. Your body changes, but you don't change at all. And that, of course, causes great confusion."

Doris Lessing

"No woman ever ages beyond 18 in her heart."

Robert A. Heinlein

"My new wife is 32 and I'm 70. She's rejuvenated me totally. It's so exciting to see life through the eyes of a modern girl."

Wilbur Smith

"Errol Flynn died on a 70-foot yacht with a 17-year-old girl. My husband's always wanted to go that way, but he's going to settle for a 17-footer and a 70-year-old."

Mary Cronkite

"It's boring to be 70, I don't want to be there, I'll be dead and gone, I don't have any aspirations to be 70…"

Freddie Mercury

"The seven ages of man: spills, drills, thrills, bills, ills, pills."

Richard John Needham

"If I had fantastic legs I might wear short skirts, but I think at 78, one's got to act one's age."

Mary Berry

"At 11, I could say 'I am sodium' (element 11) and now, at 79, I am gold."

Oliver Sacks

"Age is not measured by years. Nature does not equally distribute energy. Some people are born old and tired while others are going strong at 70."

Dorothy Thompson

"The French are true romantics. They feel the only difference between a man of 40 and one of 70 is 30 years of experience."

Maurice Chevalier

"Better pass boldly into that other world, in the full glory of some passion, than fade and wither dismally with age."

James Joyce

"At 20 a man is a peacock, at 30 a lion, at 40 a camel, at 50 a serpent, at 60 a dog, at 70 an ape, and at 80 nothing."

Baltasar Gracián

"Being over 70 is like being engaged in a war. All our friends are going or gone and we survive amongst the dead and the dying as on a battlefield."

St. Jerome

"They told me my services were no longer desired because they wanted to put in a youth programme as an advance way of keeping the club going. I'll never make the mistake of being 70 again."

Casey Stengel

"Now that I'm 78, I do tantric sex because it's very slow. My favourite position is called the plumber. You stay in all day, but nobody comes."

John Mortimer

"I can still enjoy sex at 75.
I live at 76, so it's no distance."

Bob Monkhouse

"Another good thing about being poor is that when you are 70 your children will not have declared you legally insane in order to gain control of your estate."

Woody Allen

"My grandmother is over 80 and still doesn't need glasses. Drinks right out of the bottle. "

Henry Youngman

"When you're young and beautiful,
you're paranoid and miserable. "

Helen Mirren

"Old age is not a surprise, we knew
it was coming – make the most of it.
So you may not be as fast on your
feet, and the image in your mirror
may be a little disappointing, but if
you are still functioning and not in
pain, gratitude should be the name
of the game."

Betty White

"I'm not senile. If I burn the house down it will be on purpose."

Margaret Atwood

"The good thing about being old is not being young."

Stephen Richards

"The golden age is before us, not behind us."

William Shakespeare

"Do not go gentle into that good night... rage, rage against the dying of the light."

Dylan Thomas

"Anyone who stops learning is old, whether at 20 or 80. Anyone who keeps learning stays young. The greatest thing in life is to keep your mind young."

Henry Ford

"Retirement at 65 is ridiculous.
When I was 65 I still had pimples."

George Burns

"Life would be infinitely happier
if we could only be born at the
age of 80 and gradually
approach 18."

Mark Twain

"Age does not diminish the extreme disappointment of having a scoop of ice cream fall from the cone."

Jim Fiebig

"There are three periods in life: youth, middle age and 'how well you look.'"

Nelson Rockefeller

"The age of a woman doesn't mean a thing. The best tunes are played on the oldest fiddles."

Ralph Waldo Emerson

"No woman should ever be quite accurate about her age. It looks so calculating."

Oscar Wilde

"I have reached an age when, if someone tells me to wear socks, I don't have to."

Albert Einstein

"Old Father Time will turn you into a hag if you don't show the bitch who's boss."

Mae West

"I'm not denying my age.
I'm embellishing my youth.'"

Tamara Reynolds

"Avenge yourself. Live long enough
to be a problem to your children."

Kirk Douglas

"To live beyond 80 is an exaggeration, almost an excess."

Antonio Callado

"No one should grow old who isn't ready to appear ridiculous."

John Mortimer

"My grandmother was insane. She had pierced hearing aids."

Steven Wright

"Is it me or are pensioners getting younger these days?"

The Queen Mother, aged 100

"The fountain of youth is a mixture of gin and vermouth."

Cole Porter

"When I grow up I want to be a little boy."

Joseph Heller

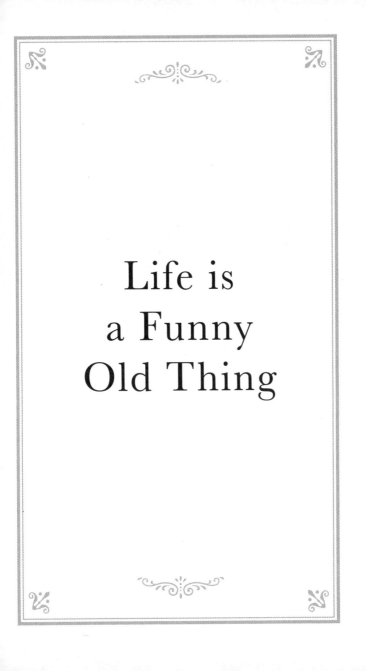

Life is
a Funny
Old Thing

"I'm 74 years old and even though I may be a bit of a rascal... 33 girls in two months seems to me too much even for a 30-year-old."

Silvio Berlusconi

"You are only young once, but you can stay immature indefinitely."

Ogden Nash

"Whatever poet, orator or sage may
say of it, old age is still old age."

Sinclair Lewis

"Be still and cool in thine
own mind and spirit."

George Fox

"I intend to live forever,
or die trying."

Groucho Marx

"Few women admit their age.
Few men act theirs."

Anon

"I still think of myself as I was
25 years ago. Then I look in
a mirror and see an old bastard
and realize it's me."

Dave Allen

"As I grow older and older
And totter towards the tomb
I find that I care less and less
Who goes to bed with whom."

Dorothy L. Sayers

"When the age is in, the wit is out."

William Shakespeare

"Age is opportunity no less than youth itself, though in another dress."

Henry Wadsworth Longfellow

"Live your life and forget your age."

Norman Vincent Peale

"I recently turned 60. Practically a third of my life is over."

Woody Allen

"Old age is like a plane flying
through a storm. Once you're
aboard, there's nothing you
can do."

Golda Meir

"You want to look younger?
Rent smaller children."

Phyllis Diller

"You're never too old to
become younger."

Mae West

"There are no old people nowadays;
they are either wonderful for their
age or dead."

Mary Pettibone Poole

"I don't feel old – I don't feel
anything until noon. Then it's
time for my nap."

Bob Hope

"I guess I don't mind so much being old, as I mind being fat and old."

Peter Gabriel

"Don't let ageing get you down. It's too hard to get back up."

John Wagner

"Middle age ends and senescence begins the day your descendants outnumber your friends."

Ogden Nash

"There is absolutely nothing to be said in favour of growing old. There ought to be legislation against it."

Patrick Moore

"People say that age is just a state of mind. I say it's more about the state of your body."

Geoffrey Parfitt

"Even if you're on the right track, you'll get run over if you just sit there."

Will Rogers

"For the first half of your life,
people tell you what you should do;
for the second half, they tell you
what you should have done."

Richard Needham

"You know you're getting old when
everything hurts. And what doesn't
hurt doesn't work."

Hy Gardner

"When I hear somebody sigh, 'Life is hard,' I am always tempted to ask, compared to what?"

Sydney Harris

"Look at the sparrows; they do not know what they will do in the next moment. Let us literally live from moment to moment."

Mahatma Gandhi

"The great thing in this world is not
so much where you stand, as in what
direction you are moving."

Oliver Wendell Holmes

"If not us, who? If not now, when?"

John F. Kennedy

"I am thankful for all of those who
said no to me. It's because of them
I'm doing it myself."

Albert Einstein

"A successful man is one who makes
more money than his wife can
spend. A successful woman is one
who can find such a man."

Lana Turner

"I always wanted to be somebody,
but now I realize I should have been
more specific."

Lily Tomlin

"I believe in rules. Sure I do.
If there weren't any rules, how
could you break them?"

Leo Durocher

"All generalizations are false,
including this one."

Mark Twain

"If two wrongs don't make
a right, try three."

Laurence J. Peter

"The only time I ever enjoyed ironing was the day I accidentally got gin in the steam iron."

Phyllis Diller

"I have a new philosophy. I'm only going to dread one day at a time."

Charles M. Schulz

"I hate housework! You make the beds, you do the dishes and six months later you have to start all over again."

Joan Rivers

"Anyone who says he can see through women is missing a lot."

Groucho Marx

"Everything I like is either illegal, immoral or fattening."

Alexander Woollcott

"My hairdresser actually spends more time digging hair out of my ears than off the top or back of my head."

Des Lynam

"I think it would be interesting if old people got anti-Alzheimer's disease where they slowly began to recover other people's lost memories."

George Carlin

"My husband has just retired. I married him for better or for worse, but not for lunch."

Hazel Weiss

"You're never too old. A person of 60 can grow as much as a child of six. Michelangelo did some of his best paintings when past 80; George Bernard Shaw was still writing plays at 90; Grandma Moses didn't even begin painting until she was 79."

Maxwell Naltz

"Old age is like underwear. It creeps up on you."

Lois L. Kaufman

"The older I get, the older old is."

Tom Baker

"Harrison Ford may be getting
old, but he can still fight like
a 28-year-old man."

Harrison Ford

"It's very ageing to talk about age."

Merle Oberon

"No spring, nor summer hath such grace as I have seen in one autumnal face."

John Donne

"My grandkids believe I'm the oldest thing in the world. And after two or three hours with them, I believe it, too."

Gene Perret

"The reason people blame things
on the previous generation is that
there's only one other choice."

Doug Larson

"Retirement homes are great.
It's like being a baby, only you're
old enough to appreciate it."

Homer Simpson

"I have been asked to pose for *Penthouse* on my hundredth birthday. Everybody is going to be sorry."

Dolly Parton

"I complain that the years fly past, but then I look in a mirror and see that very few of them actually got past."

Robert Brault

"If you live to be one hundred,
you've got it made. Very few people
die past that age."

George Burns

"I don't need you to remind
me of my age. I have a bladder
to do that for me."

Stephen Fry

"The older I grow, the more
I distrust the familiar doctrine
that age brings wisdom."

H. L. Mencken

"One should never trust a woman
who tells one her real age. A woman
who would tell one that would tell
one anything."

Oscar Wilde

"My idea of hell is to be
young again."

Marge Piercy

"When it comes to staying young,
a mind-lift beats a face-lift any day."

Marty Bucella

"Life is a moderately good play with
a badly written third act."

Truman Capote

Mind, Body and Soul

"How body from spirit slowly
does unwind, until we are pure
spirit at the end."

Theodore Roethke

"After 30, a body has a
mind of its own."

Bette Midler

"It is sad to grow old,
but nice to ripen."

Brigitte Bardot

"Regrets are the natural
property of grey hairs."

Charles Dickens

"It's not how old you are,
it's how you are old."

Jules Renard

"Millions long for immortality
who do not know what to do
with themselves on a rainy
Sunday afternoon."

Susan Ertz

"There is only one cure for
grey hair. It was invented
by a Frenchman. It is called
the guillotine."

P. G. Wodehouse

"I have finally come to the
conclusion that a good reliable set
of bowels is worth more to man
than any quantity of brains."

Josh Billings

"My dad says finding somebody that when you are old is going to wipe your arse – that's marriage."

Jason Manford

"My granny wore a hearing aid that was always tuned too low, because when she turned it up, it whistled, and every dog in Dublin rushed to her side."

Terry Wogan

"They tell you that you'll lose your mind when you grow older. What they don't tell you is that you won't miss it very much."

Malcolm Cowley

"When I turn my hearing aid up to ten, I can hear a canary break wind six miles away."

Sophia Petrillo, The Golden Girls

"A glass of wine with lunch?
Is that wise? You know you
have to reign all afternoon."

The Queen Mother to Queen Elizabeth II

"The advantages of dating younger
men is that on them everything, like
hair and teeth, is in the right place
as opposed to being on the bedside
table or bathroom floor."

Candace Bushnell

"Hugh Hefner now has seven girlfriends – one for each day of the week. Someone needs to tell him that those are nurses."

Jay Leno

"To keep the heart unwrinkled, to be hopeful, kindly, cheerful, reverent – that is to triumph over old age."

Thomas Bailey Aldrich

"Cherish all your happy
moments: they make a fine
cushion for old age."

Christopher Morley

"'Old' is not a dirty word. Old age
is not an illness. It took a long time
and a lot of hard work to get here
and I see no reason to apologise
for my arrival."

Irma Kurtz

"There is a fountain of youth:
it is your mind, your talents, the
creativity you bring to your life and
the lives of the people you love.
When you learn to tap this source,
you will have truly defeated age."

Sophia Loren

"It's not that age brings childhood
back again, age merely shows what
children we remain."

Johann Wolfgang von Goethe

"Wrinkles should merely indicate where smiles have been."

Mark Twain

"Age does not protect you from love. But love, to some extent, protects you from age."

Anaïs Nin

"You can't help getting older, but you don't have to get old."

George Burns

"Youth is the gift of nature,
but age is a work of art."

Stanislaw Jerzy Lec

"Age appears to be best in four
things: old wood best to burn, old
wine to drink, old friends to trust
and old authors to read."

Francis Bacon

"I don't believe one grows older.
I think that what happens early on
in life is that at a certain age one
stands still and stagnates."

T. S. Eliot

"I'm not interested in age. People
who tell me their age are silly.
You're as old as you feel."

Henri Frédéric Amiel

"An archaeologist is the best husband a woman can have. The older she gets the more interested he is in her."

Agatha Christie

"The really frightening thing about middle age is the knowledge that you'll grow out of it."

Doris Day

"Age is a high price to pay for maturity."

Tom Stoppard

"Growing old is mandatory;
growing up is optional."

Chili Davis

"People under 24 think old age
starts around 55, those over 75, on
the other hand, believe that youth
doesn't end until the age of 58."

Alexander Chancellor

"You can live to be a hundred if you give up all things that make you want to live to be a hundred."

Woody Allen

"Everything slows down with age, except the time it takes cake and ice cream to reach your hips."

John Wagner

"As you get older three things happen. The first is your memory goes, and I can't remember the other two."

Norman Wisdom

"Old age isn't so bad when you consider the alternative."

Maurice Chevalier

"Those who love deeply never grow old; they may die of old age, but they die young."

Dorothy Canfield Fisher

"The idea is to die young as late as possible."

Ashley Montagu

"When you are dissatisfied and would like to go back to youth, think of algebra."

Will Rogers

"Let us never know what old age
is. Let us know the happiness time
brings, not count the years."

Ausonius

"The secret of staying young is
to live honestly, eat slowly and
lie about your age."

Lucille Ball

"The great thing about getting older
is that you don't lose all the other
ages you've been."

Madeleine L'Engle

"Some men like shiny new toys.
Others like the priceless antique."

Donna Lynn Hope

"How far away the stars seem, and
how far is our first kiss, and ah, how
old my heart."

W. B. Yeats

"You can't turn back the clock.
But you can wind it up again."

Bonnie Prudden

"I don't want to die an old lady."

Edith Piaf

"The line between angry young
woman and grumpy old lady
is very fine."

Judy Horacek

"Imperfection is beauty, madness
is genius and it's better to be
absolutely ridiculous than
absolutely boring."

Marilyn Monroe

"I can honestly say I love getting older. Then again, I never put my glasses on before looking in the mirror."

Cherie Lunghi

"I knew I was getting old when the Pope started looking young."

Billy Wilder

"I don't plan to grow old
gracefully. I plan to have facelifts
until my ears meet."

Rita Rudner

"I'm at an age when my back
goes out more than I do."

Phyllis Diller

"There are three classes into which all the women past 70 that ever I knew were to be divided: 1. That dear old soul; 2. That old woman; 3. That old witch."

Samuel Taylor Coleridge

"Let us respect grey hairs, especially our own."

J. P. Sears

"The spiritual eyesight improves as the physical eyesight declines."

Plato

"As you get older, you don't get as horny – I don't take as many cold showers a day as I used to."

Tom Jones

"What is a younger woman? I'm pretty old, so almost every woman is younger than me."

Jack Nicholson

"After a man passes 60, his mischief is mainly in his head."

Washington Irving

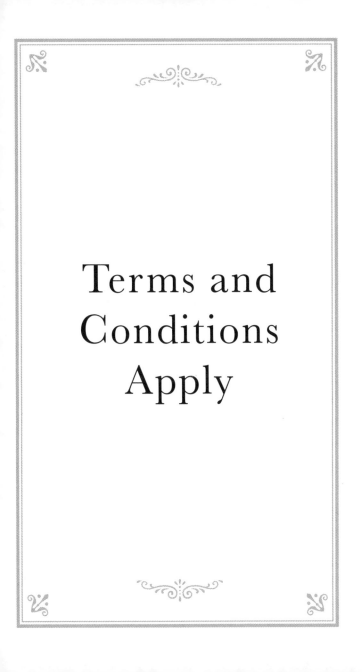

Terms and Conditions Apply

"Old age isn't a battle;
old age is a massacre."

Philip Roth

"I think ageing has nothing to
recommend it. You don't gain any
wisdom as the years go by. You fall
apart, is what happens. People try
and put a nice varnish on it, and
say, well, you mellow. You come to
understand life and accept things.
But you'd trade all of that for
being 35 again."

Woody Allen

"No man loves life like him that's growing old."

Sophocles

"The old are in a second childhood."

Aristophanes

"I truly believe that age – if you're healthy – age is just a number."

Hugh Hefner

"There is this difference between the grief of youth and that of old age: youth's burden is lightened by as much of it as another shares; old age may give and give, but the sorrow remains the same."

O. Henry

"The disappointment of manhood succeeds to the delusion of youth: let us hope that the heritage of old age is not despair."

Benjamin Disraeli

"Old age is the most unexpected
of all the things that can
happen to a man."

Leon Trotsky

"What is the worst of woes
that wait on age?
What stamps the wrinkle
deeper on the brow?
To view each loved one
blotted from life's page,
And be alone on earth,
as I am now."

Lord Byron

"Age overtakes us all;
our temples first; then
on o'er cheek and chin,
slowly and surely, creep
the frosts of time.
Up and do somewhat,
ere thy limbs are sere."

Theocritus

"The pleasures that once were
heaven, look silly at 67."

Noel Coward

"The secret of a good old
age is simply an honorable
pact with solitude."

Gabriel García Márquez

"Old men's eyes are like old men's
memories; they are strongest for
things a long way off."

George Eliot

"I have so many liver spots, I ought
to come with a side of onions."

Phyllis Diller

"Age is foolish and forgetful when it
underestimates youth."

J. K. Rowling

"If you can't have fun as an ageing sex symbol when you hit 60, I don't know what will become of you."

Raquel Welch

"The only real change in life comes with the consciousness of old age."

Austin O'Malley

"Before 40 we live forwards;
after 40 we live backwards."

Charles Edward Jerningham

"I only take Viagra when I am
with more than one woman."

Jack Nicholson

"Nothing makes one old so
quickly as the ever-present thought
that one is growing older."

Georg Christoph Lichtenberg

"Nothing makes you look older
than attempting to look young."

Karl Lagerfeld

"In youth all doors open outward;
in old age all open inward."

Henry Wadsworth Longfellow

"I'm like a good cheese.
I'm just getting mouldy enough
to be interesting."

Paul Newman

"Whenever a man's friends begin
to compliment him about looking
young, he may be sure that they
think he is growing old."

Washington Irving

"Growing old is no more than
a bad habit a busy man has
no time to form."

André Maurois

"What's a man's age? He must hurry more, that's all; Cram in a day what his youth took a year to hold."

Robert Browning

"I am really looking forward as I get older and older to being less and less nice."

Annette Bening

"The world's oldest woman passed
away at 116. They keep dying.
I think that title may be cursed."

David Letterman

"White hair often covers the
head, but the heart that holds
it is ever young."

Honoré De Balzac

"You're only given a little spark of madness. You mustn't lose it."

Robin Williams

"Since people are going to be living longer and getting older, they'll just have to learn how to be babies longer."

Andy Warhol

"I am at that age. Too young for the bowling green, too old for Ecstasy."

Rab C. Nesbitt

"Old men are dangerous: it doesn't matter to them what is going to happen to the world."

George Bernard Shaw

"There's nothing like being old to be sure of everything."

Fran Lebowitz

"Even though you're growing up, you should never stop having fun."

Nina Dobrev

"I love everything that's old:
old friends, old times, old manners,
old books, old wines."

Oliver Goldsmith

"We grow too soon old and
too late smart."

Dutch proverb

"Youth is happy because it has the ability to see beauty. Anyone who keeps the ability to see beauty never grows old."

Franz Kafka

"Men are like wine. Some turn to vinegar, but the best improve with age."

C. E. M. Joad

"The older the fiddle,
the sweeter the tune."

Irish proverb

"Moisturizers do work. The rest
is pap. There is nothing on God's
earth that will take away 30 years of
arguing with your husband."

Anita Roddick

"There seem to be two main types of people in the world, crosswords and sudokus."

Rebecca McKinsey

"I am getting to an age when I can only enjoy the last sport left. It is called hunting for your spectacles."

Edward Grey

"I am old enough to see how little
I have done in so much time, and
how much I have to do in so little."

Sheila Kaye-Smith

"Don't be afraid your life will end;
be afraid that it will never begin."

Grace Hansen

"The life expectancy now is 72 for men, and 75 or 76 or something for women. It's amazing to think that just a couple of thousands of years ago, life expectancy was 30, which in our terms would be that you get your driver's licence around 5, get married at 9, divorced at 15, in your late teens move down to Florida."

Jerry Seinfeld

"Mistakes are part of the dues that
one pays for a full life."

Sophia Loren

"Being old isn't something to deny,
hush up or apologise for.
It's something to celebrate."

Virginia Ironside

"The reason grandchildren and
grandparents get along so well is
that they have a common enemy."

Sam Levenson

Seventy Ain't
for Sissies

"Getting old ain't for sissies."

Betty Davis

"Money isn't everything, but
it sure keeps you in touch with
your children."

J. Paul Getty

"I don't want to retire. I'm not that
good at crossword puzzles."

Norman Mailer

"The key to a successful marriage
is to argue naked."

LeAnn Rimes

"Your kids will forgive you someday.
Of course, by then you'll be dead."

Sophia Petrillo, The Golden Girls

"Don't ever save anything for
a special occasion. Being alive
is the special occasion."

Avril Sloe

"Grow old along with me!
The best is yet to be,
The last of life, for which the first
was made:
Our times are in His hand
Who saith, 'A whole I planned,
Youth shows but half; trust God: see
all, nor be afraid!"

Robert Browning

"When you are old and grey
and full of sleep,
And nodding by the fire,
take down this book,
And slowly read, and dream
of the soft look
Your eyes had once, and of
their shadows deep."

W. B. Yeats

"Like many women my age,
I am 28 years old."

Neil Gaiman

"Old age is always wakeful; as if,
the longer linked with life, the less
man has to do with aught that
looks like death."

Herman Melville

"If I had known I was going to live this long, I would have taken better care of myself."

Mae West

"The secret to old age: you have to know what you're going to do the next day."

Louis J. Lefkowitz

"The old believe everything,
the middle-aged suspect everything,
the young know everything."

Oscar Wilde

"Age is an issue of mind over
matter. If you don't mind,
it doesn't matter."

Mark Twain

"You don't stop laughing because you grow older. You grow older because you stop laughing."

Maurice Chevalier

"Old age, believe me, is a good and pleasant thing. It is true you are gently shouldered off the stage, but then you are given such a comfortable front stall as spectator."

Confucius

"Age is not important unless
you're a cheese."

Helen Hayes

"In youth we run into difficulties.
In old age difficulties run into us."

Beverly Sills

"I don't feel old. I don't feel
anything till noon. That's when
it's time for my nap. "

Bob Hope

"There are two lasting bequests we can give our children. One is roots. The other is wings."

Hodding Carter, Jr.

"Inside every old person is a young person wondering what happened."

Terry Pratchett

"Birthdays are good for you. Statistics show that the people who have the most live the longest."

Larry Lorenzoni

"I don't want to achieve immortality through my work, I want to achieve it through not dying."

Woody Allen

"The key to successful ageing is to pay as little attention to it as possible."

Judith Regan

"What most persons consider as virtue, after the age of 40 is simply a loss of energy."

Voltaire

"I'm like old wine. They don't bring me out very often, but I'm well preserved."

Rose Kennedy

"My first advice on how not to grow old would be to choose you ancestors carefully."

Bertrand Russell

"You are not permitted to kill a woman who has injured you, but nothing forbids you to reflect that she is growing older every minute. You are avenged 1,440 times a day."

Ambrose Bierce

"Old age comes on suddenly
and not gradually as is thought."

Emily Dickinson

"I think your whole life shows
in your face and you should
be proud of that."

Lauren Bacall

"For those of you who don't have grandchildren, get some. Get them on eBay if you have to."

Diahann Carroll

"Some day you will be old enough to start reading fairy tales again."

C. S. Lewis

"Just remember, when you're
over the hill, you begin to
pick up speed."

Charles M. Schulz

"I don't believe in ageing.
I believe in forever altering
one's aspect to the sun."

Virginia Woolf

"A sexagenarian?
At his age?
That's disgusting"

Gracie Allen

"Too many people, when they
get old, think that they have to
live by the calendar."

John Glenn

"When people talk about the good old days, I say to people, 'It's not the days that are old, it's you that's old.' I hate the good old days. What is important is that today is good."

Karl Lagerfeld

"Do not try to live forever, you will not succeed."

George Bernard Shaw

"By the time you're 80 years old you've learned everything. You only have to remember it."

George Burns

"He who is of a calm and happy nature will hardly feel the pressure of age, but to him who is of an opposite disposition, youth and age are equally a burden."

Plato

"The wiser mind mourns less for
what age takes away than what it
leaves behind."

William Wordsworth

"To know how to grow old is
the master work of wisdom,
and one of the most difficult
chapters in the great art of living."

Henri Frederic Amiel

"To keep the heart
unwrinkled, to be hopeful,
kindly, cheerful, reverent, that
is to triumph over old age."

Thomas B. Aldrich

"You can only perceive real beauty
in a person as they get older."

Anouk Aimée

"For all the advances in
medicine, there is still no cure
for the common birthday."

John Glenn

"Age is strictly a case of
mind over matter. If you don't
mind, it doesn't matter."

Jack Benny

"Old age is great trial. One has to be so damned *good!*"

May Sarton

"You will recognize, my boy, the first sign of old age: it is when you go out into the streets of London and realize for the first time how young the policemen look."

Sir Seymour Hicks

"What could be more beautiful than a dear old lady growing wise with age? Every age can be enchanting, provided you live within it."

Brigitte Bardot

"May you live all the days of your life."

Jonathan Swift

"The best birthdays of all are those that haven't arrived yet."

Robert Orben

"Inside every older person is a younger person wondering what the hell happened."

Cora Harvey Armstrong

"I am long on ideas, but short on time. I expect to live to be only about a hundred."

Thomas Edison

"Time flies like an arrow. Fruit flies like a banana."

Groucho Marx

"Take care of your body. It's the
only place you have to live."

Jim Rohn

"Youth is the time for adventures
of the body, but age for the
triumphs of the mind."

Logan Pearsall Smith

"The tragedy of old age is not that
one is old, but that one is young."

Oscar Wilde

"Backward, turn backward,
O Time, in your flight. Make me a
child again just for tonight! "

Elizabeth Akers Allen

"And in the end, it's not the years in your life that count. It's the life in your years."

Abraham Lincoln

"Nobody grows old merely by living a number of years. We grow old by deserting our ideals. Years may wrinkle the skin, but to give up enthusiasm wrinkles the soul."

Samuel Ullman

"Youth is a disease from
which we all recover."

Dorothy Fulheim

"First you forget names, then you
forget faces, then you forget to pull
your zipper up, then you forget to
pull your zipper down."

Leo Rosenberg

"You're never too old.
Unfortunately, you're always
too young to know it."

Robert Brault

"We turn not older with years,
but newer every day."

Emily Dickinson

"You know you've lived a
few years when you start having
your second thoughts first."

Robert Brault

"Time moves in one direction,
memory in another."

William Gibson

"Older women are best, because they always think they may be doing it for the last time."

Ian Fleming

"If I had known how wonderful it would be to have grandchildren, I'd have had them first."

Lois Wyse

"Children are a great comfort in your old age. And they help you reach it faster, too."

Lionel Kaufman

"They told me that grandchildren are the reward you get for not killing your children."

Virginia Ironside

"You only live once, but if you
do it right, once is enough."

Mae West

"And the beauty of a woman,
with passing years, only grows!"

Audrey Hepburn

"As one grows older, one becomes
wiser and more foolish."

François de la Rochefoucauld

"We do not count a man's years
until he has nothing else to count."

Ralph Waldo Emerson

"There's one more terrifying
fact about old people: I'm going
to be one soon."

P. J. O'Rourke

"Getting older is no problem.
You just have to live long enough."

Groucho Marx

"The great thing about getting older
is that you get a chance to tell the
people in your life who matter what
they mean to you."

Mike Love

"Let's face it, a nice creamy
chocolate cake does a lot for a
lot of people; it does for me."

Audrey Hepburn

"Life is full of misery, loneliness and suffering – and it's all over much too soon."

Woody Allen

"A comfortable old age is the reward of a well-spent youth. Instead of its bringing sad and melancholy prospects of decay, it would give us hopes of eternal youth in a better world."

Lydia M. Child

"No one is so old as to think he cannot live one more year."

Marcus T. Cicero

"Age is something that doesn't matter, unless you are a cheese."

Billie Burke

"Ageing seems to be the only available way to live a long life."

Daniel Francois Esprit Auber

"Old age is like everything else.
To make a success of it, you've
got to start young."

Fred Astaire

"We are always the
same age inside."

Gertrude Stein

"Youth has no age."

Pablo Picasso

"The secret of genius is to carry the spirit of the child into old age, which means never losing your enthusiasm."

Aldous Huxley

"Wives are young men's mistresses, companions for middle age and old men's nurses."

Francis Bacon

"Setting a good example for your children takes all the fun out of middle age."

William Feather

"Be eccentric now. Don't wait for old age to wear purple."

Regina Brett

"Age to women is like kryptonite to Superman."

Kathy Lette

"Learning is an ornament in prosperity, a refuge in adversity and a provision in old age."

Aristotle